# ·C·O·N·T·E·N·T·S·

# INTRODUCTION

Drawing accurate statistical charts requires careful planning and execution. The following pages will help you develop a professional approach to information design.

ON THE
·S·P·O·T·
GUIDES

**This book is to be returned on or before the last date stamped below.**

## AN OUTLINE PRESS BOOK

© TREVOR BOUNFORD 1991
First published in Great Britain in 1991 by
Outline Press (Book Publishers) Limited
115J Cleveland Street
London W1P 5PN

### ISBN 1.871547.11.3

This book was designed and produced by
Chapman Bounford and Associates for
THE OUTLINE PRESS

Printed and bound by Regent, Hong Kong

Diagrammatic forms of representation have always been used to convey basic facts and comparative data. The earliest forms of written communication were based on simple graphic symbols and images. In the modern world, a graphic image can still convey certain types of information more immediately and economically than the written word and its 'language' can be universally understood. Although words may be required to supplement or elaborate the graphic image, these can be very simple, concise and direct.

It is remarkable that in this age of sophisticated communications technology, simple diagrammatic representation remains a vital tool. Skilfully constructed, a chart or diagram conveys complex information quickly and clearly. Maps, diagrams and charts, in a variety of forms, have become an essential part of our everyday life. Printed media including newspapers, magazines, books and the electronic media of television, film and computer all make use of these means of communication - to greater and lesser degrees of success. But, with one or two exceptions, there have been few highly skilled exponents of this practical artform. All too often a chart or diagram that could have been useful has been rendered useless by unskilled execution.

This book is a practical guide for anyone who wishes to employ basic information graphics. It introduces methods of ordering and presenting statistical information via simple but effective graphic forms. An ability to use basic studio equipment has been assumed. It is helpful to make a rough plot of a chart on graph paper to see the 'shape' of the data before starting an accurate plot. Use good quality tracing paper for the final plot. This will remain stable and not distort with humidity. It also allows you to trace over graph paper or existing plots.

Although construction of the charts is described as a manual drawing process, the instructions can be easily adapted to working with drawing programmes on a computer.

## STATISTICAL CHARTS

There are several basic ways of presenting statistical information in chart form. What all charts have in common is the portrayal of a relationship, a similarity, difference or pattern, of comparative values – there is no point in drawing one datum (point of value) if there is no other to compare that value with. The general types of chart are described below in their basic forms.

### Line graph

The line graph shows the relationship of variable points of value plotted on two regular comparative scales. The horizontal scale usually represents time – the hours, months, years etc. over which the data measurements have been made. The vertical scale usually represents the regular value scale of the datum points – dollars, tonnes, miles etc. Lines drawn directly from datum point to datum point show the rate of increase or decrease when compared to the horizontal grid line.

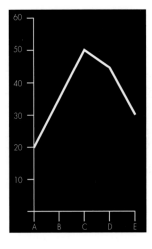

### Bar chart

The basic bar chart is similar to the line graph but stresses comparisons of absolute values rather than degree of change. The lengths or heights of the bars show the specific quantities.

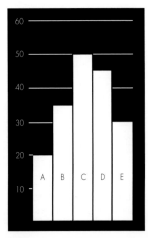

## Area chart

Whereas the length of each bar in a bar chart represents a value, the width of the bar having little or no relevance, area charts compare values by area. This means that both the length and width are significant in the calculation. Area charts are particularly useful when comparing values which vary greatly. For example, if comparing values of 25 and 49 one bar would need to be almost twice as long as the other in a bar chart, but the values could be shown by areas of 5 x 5 and 7 x 7 in an area chart.

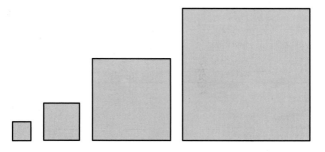

## Pie chart

This is a variation of the area chart but is the most common type in regular use. It is used to demonstrate the relative proportions of a whole – represented by the area of a circle. The subdividing lines radiate from the centre of the circle in the way that a pie or cake might be sliced into portions (hence the name).

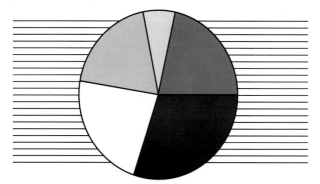

These are the most popular forms of statistical chart. They can be used in their basic form or can be enhanced to make them more striking or decorative. They can also be combined or subdivided to include more complex data.

## CHOOSING A STATISTICAL CHART

Although there are no fixed rules in selecting and applying any chart, there are some conventions, largely based on commonsense, which should be considered.

● Don't make comparisons which are not of the same context. For example, it would be misleading to show the working male population of one country but compare it to the total working population of another, or to take the population of one country in 1970 and compare it with the population of another in 1990, unless a particular point is being made and the discrepancy is highlighted.

● Don't 'bury' the information. The point of the diagram is to enable the reader to see quickly and draw some conclusion. Over-elaborating the design may confuse or distort the information.

● Make labels and other annotation clear and unambiguous.

● If the diagram doesn't convey the information as effectively as possible – making it more easily assimilated than it would be in words, and of immediate graphic impact – rethink the presentation or reconsider whether a diagram is really necessary.

● Bear in mind the user – a logarithmic axis on a multiple split-bar chart may be too sophisticated for general readership. An over-simplified visual statement may be unnecessary and uninspiring for a highly technical audience.

To some extent these decisions are editorial and the designer will have been given data to work with. Nevertheless one should avoid misleading comparisons as the visualized statement is intended to create an impact.

### Which chart?

Choosing the right chart for the job is often a matter of taste. Most data could be shown in graph or bar chart, the space available may help to determine which to use. Pie charts, being circular, occupy a squarer shape, although not necessarily, as will be shown later. The pie chart is used specifically to show the breakdown of a total value. Such data could also be shown by a bar, or area chart. Bar charts can be extended to exaggerate differences between values shown by lengths of bars. Graphs can also be 'stretched' but this can sometimes appear visually uncomfortable.
It is easier to incorporate data labels on bar charts than on line graphs and this in itself may determine the choice.

## Data

This book can only provide a rudimentary understanding of data analysis. (Note that the word 'data' is plural, and the singular 'datum' is used frequently.) The user should be clear about the data being used.

● Make sure that the reference from which you are working is quite legible and that values are consistent. If it is necessary to convert values from one sort of unit to another (temperature in degrees Fahrenheit to degrees Celsius for example) be sure to understand the relationship − some useful conversion tables are included at the end of this book.

● Always have the data approved before creating final artwork. It may not be possible to amend the drawing to include changed or additional data, in which case the diagram will have to be drawn again.

● Use only conventional abbreviations for units, particularly when using scientific data and especially if preparing charts in another language.

● Watch out for any particularly large values that have to be compared to small values. It may be that a relevant part of the 'story' is contained in this discrepancy but you may also need to show some very small differences on the same chart. Using two charts, one to focus on the smaller differences and one to show the overall pattern, may be a better solution than trying to show both on one. A few suggestions are given for combining longer and shorter elements in a single chart.

● Do not try to include too much data in each diagram. The well-designed chart can present a great amount of data in a way that enables the user to extract 'pictures' of the information. But a chart overloaded with information will only confuse and obscure. It may be better to use two or more charts to highlight several important issues. This is particularly important where the diagrams are to be projected as part of a slide series or as an OHP presentation and will therefore not be displayed for long. In this case charts need to be particularly direct and to the point, with clear labelling.

## Tables

It may not always be appropriate to use a chart or diagram to present data. Particularly complex or detailed data might be better shown typographically in tabular form. In fact sometimes it is useful to use both, with the diagram making the specific point and tabular data giving a broader background.

## TIPS AND TECHNIQUES

Knowledge of basic drawing techniques is essential in order to create neat and accurate artwork. Even when using a computer to create charts, basic drafting ability is useful. To plot and draw diagrams successfully use good quality, properly functioning equipment. Fine-leaded clutch-type pencils are more reliable than wooden ones. Technical pens, available in a variety of precise nib sizes, are excellent for maintaining constant line widths. Set-squares, a protractor, a straight-edge and an eraser are also vital. Also very useful are graph paper, a basic calculator, typographic depth-scale, circle and ellipse templates. A drawing board with precision parallel motion is well worth the investment. Keep all implements clean and well maintained.

### Calculator

The calculator is a very useful device for accurate chart calculation. Most have much the same working method and have handy additional functions.

● Entering a value and pressing the + button twice, for example, activates a 'constant addition' function which adds the first number to the total each time the = button is pressed.
22.4 ++ = 44.8 = 67.2 = 89.6 = 112 etc.

● This also works with the −, x and ÷ buttons but be sure to key numbers in the correct sequence. 2 xx 3 gives the sequence:
6  12  24  48  96 etc. (twice the answer each time)
but 3 xx 2 gives:
6  18  54  162  486 etc. (three times the answer).

● To constantly halve values, key in 2 followed by ÷÷ then the total value, for example:
2 ÷÷ 96 = 48 = 24 = 12 = 6 = 3 = 1.5 etc.

● A memory storage function is also useful, as is a square root key (for working out areas of circles etc.) and a percentage function.

● Make a percentage increase to a value as follows: key the value, then press the x key then the % key and immediately press the + key, this automatically adds the percentage value to the original amount.
120 x 20 % + (will show the total of 144).

● The memory function is useful for multiplying or dividing by a constant factor. To convert inches to centimetres, for example, key in the value 2.54 (1 inch = 2.54 centimetres) and press the M+ key. Then key in the first of the inch measurements, press x, then press MR followed by = to obtain the converted value. Do this for each inch value, taking care not to press the M+ key.

## Techniques for measuring length

It is unlikely that data and chart area conveniently coincide with a ruler measurement. Usually lengths need to be calculated and plotted. There are several short-cuts which can be employed.

The following methods are based on a total available length/width of 82mm (the column width of this page) and a data set of 172.6, 115, 80.7 and 55 units (these units could be miles, hours, dollars or anything else – the actual unit is irrelevant).

**Calculator and ruler method** Clear the calculator memory. Divide 82 on the calculator by 172.6 to obtain the conversion factor, 0.475. Store this value in the calculator memory. Multiply 115 by 0.475 (115 x MR) to calculate the equivalent line length in millimetres, 54.6. Do the same for the other numbers; 80.7 = 38.3 and 55 = 26.1. These measurements can now be marked off against the ruler.

**Typescale method** A standard typographer's depth scale has measurements based on typographic point sizes that may provide a useful alternative to metric or imperial measures. Here 17.26 ems on the 13.5 point scale equals 82mm. Using 17.26 as 172.6, your highest datum in the set, you can measure off the others on the scale.

**Angled set-square method** It is possible to divide any given length proportionally using a ruler and set-square, without the need for any form of mathematical calculation. With this method you can create a temporary 'ruler' on a sheet of paper – a measurement scale relating to the particular job in hand.

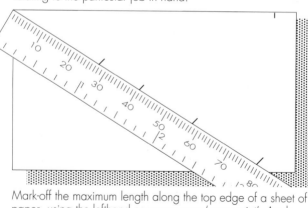

Mark-off the maximum length along the top edge of a sheet of paper, using the lefthand corner as your 'zero point'. Angle the ruler downward from the zero point and draw a line. On this line you will measure off your data points, using any easily read measurement to correspond to the unit value.

In this example the line is to be divided corresponding to the unit values of 172.6, 115, 80.7 and 55. The final datum point on the angled line should fall as closely as possible below the end point at the paper's top edge. To produce an accurate and easily readable conversion that fits within the paper width, the units are halved and translated into millimetre measurements:

172.6 units = 86.3mm; 115 units = 57.5mm;
80.7 units = 40.3mm; 55 units = 27.5mm.
Mark off these measurements along the angled line on the paper.

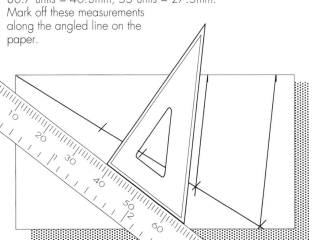

Starting at the last datum point, position the long edge of a set-square to join this point with the end point at the paper's top edge. Draw a connecting line between them. Place a ruler along the lower edge of the set-square and slide the ruler to the next datum point. Draw the line from that point to the paper's edge.

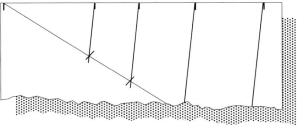

Draw lines from each of the data points in the same way making sure the ruler doesn't slip. When complete, the edge of the paper forms a 'ruler' marked with the required proportional measurement scale.

You can use the same method to divide an arbitrary length into equal divisions, by marking off the divisions on the angled line and projecting them upward as before.

## USING PERSPECTIVE

Charts drawn in perspective can produce some interesting, even dramatic effects. Perspective is particularly useful for compressing information within a confined space. However the technique should be used with caution as the data can become substantially distorted.

### Constructing a perspective grid

A basic understanding of perspective is useful, but a simple perspective grid can be easily constructed as follows.

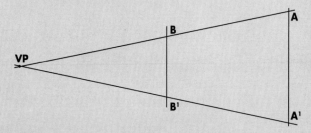

Draw two parallel vertical lines to represent the left and right sides of the grid. Then establish a vanishing point (VP) to the left of the lefthand vertical at a distance that gives a satisfactory degree of foreshortening (some trial and error may be necessary). Mark the top and bottom of the right hand vertical (A:A'), then join these points to the vanishing point. Where these lines cut through the left vertical mark the points B and B'.
● This figure, A:A':B:B', is a trapezium, and appears to be a rectangle foreshortened by perspective.

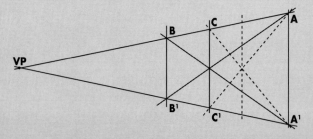

Draw lines from each corner to its diagonal opposite – A to B' and B to A'. Where these lines intersect is the plotted centre of the figure and a vertical line, C:C', can be drawn through this point. This creates two new trapezia, which can be divided by the same method. These four can also be sub-divided and so on until the desired number of divisions is achieved.

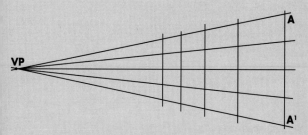

The horizontal divisions are plotted by dividing the line A:A′ into the requisite number of divisions and drawing these across the first trapezium to align with the vanishing point.

## Dividing the grid

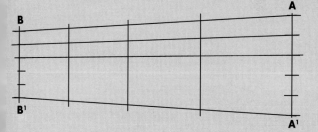

A vanishing point is useful but not necessary as once a basic trapezium has been drawn and the vertical lines plotted, the horizontal grid can be drawn by measuring and marking on both A:A′ and B:B′ and joining the corresponding points.

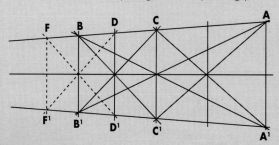

To plot an uneven number of vertical divisions either establish B:B′ beyond the required lefthand edge or plot an additional trapezium as shown above by drawing the horizontal centre line through to the vanishing point and drawing diagonals from D and D′ through the centre of B:B′ to cut the top and bottom lines at F and F′. Join these two points to complete the extension.

# LINE GRAPHS

The line graph shows the relationship between two or more points of value, on a drawn or implied grid, and the amount of decrease and increase between those points. It requires at least two sets of data, one expressing the values and another showing a time period or some other regular scale along which the first values are to be compared.

## THE BASIC CHART

This set of data shows comparative levels of production of a business at quarterly intervals over a twelve month period.

December 1995, 24 units; March 1996, 72 units; June 1996, 89 units; September 1996, 19 units; December 1996, 33 units.

This list could be arranged as a simple table.

| Quarter | Dec | Mar | Jun | Sep | Dec |
|---|---|---|---|---|---|
| Year | 1995 | 1996 | 1996 | 1996 | 1996 |
| Units | 24 | 72 | 89 | 19 | 33 |

The table shows the linear structure of the timescale but gives no visual indication of the relative values. If the data are repositioned as points on a vertical scale the picture is clearer.

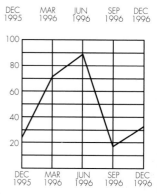

By drawing lines between the points an indication of the rate of change is shown. With the addition of background grid and scale the individual point labels may be eliminated.

The scales against which the data points on the graph are plotted are known as axes. The vertical axis is designated the Y-axis. The horizontal axis is known as the X-axis.

## CONSTRUCTING A LINE GRAPH

The general shape of the line graph depends upon the number of data points to be fitted to the X- and Y-axes and the relative scale of values contained within the data. If you have a given area within which the graph is to be drawn, you first need to calculate how much of that area can be given over to the graph itself and what proportion of the space may be required for labelling the axes with their unit value.

The following example shows how to create a simple graph based on five points of data:

```
Exports (in thousand US dollars)
Dec 1995              $  95
Mar 1996              $ 250
June 1996$ 142
Sep 1996              $ 330
Dec 1996              $ 292
```

The Y-axis (vertical) must show the unit value being used – US dollars (thousands) – and the numerical values – 95, 250, 142, 330, 292. You need to estimate the width of a lefthand margin that can accommodate this annotation.

Labels on the X-axis (horizontal) designating the time period can be neatly abbreviated, but depending on the width of the graph overall and divisions between data points, each reference of month/year may need to be split onto two lines to fit widthways.

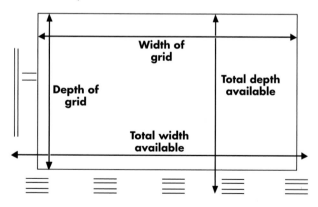

Mark out the overall area for the graph artwork and allow the estimated depth at side and base for the labelling.

Note that the first datum point on the X-axis corresponds to the base of the Y-axis, so there are five datum points but four equal divisions of the X-axis are required.

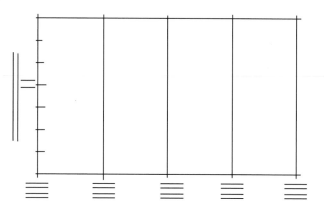

Divide the X-axis into four, either by calculating the divisions if it is a simple sum, or by using the angled set-square method (see pages 14 and 15).

To calculate the division of the Y-axis, decide on the highest value that should be represented, which will form the top line of the grid. As the highest unit value in the data is 330 it is sensible to put the top line at 350 and create seven 50-unit divisions.

If you cannot accurately measure these divisions on a ruler or typescale, use a calculator to divide the actual height of the grid in millimetres by the total number of units on the Y-axis scale (350). Use the answer as a conversion factor to calculate the height of the grid divisions and the data points, all of which can be plotted on the chart.

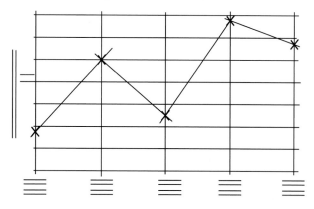

Draw the horizontal rules for the grid divisions and, having plotted the data, join up the points to complete the graph line.

## Adding labels

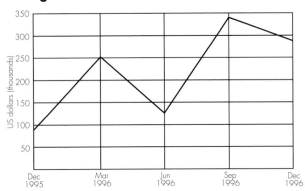

If the graph is satisfactory, the lines can be inked in with a technical pen, or made up from dry-transfer rule. Labels are added in their planned positions. Positioning of labels is a matter of common sense and taste.

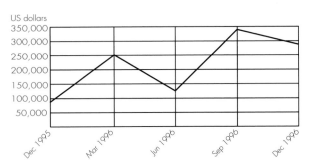

This example shows how annotation can be varied on the graph (adjust the shape at the planning stage).

## Adjusting the shape of the graph

Varying the width of the graph will compress or expand the graph line. The compressed graph line emphasizes differences between data.

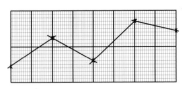
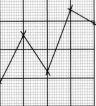

## GRAPHIC VARIATIONS

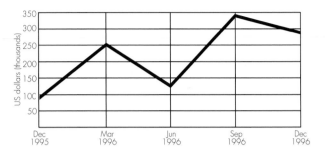

A heavier line gives emphasis but be sure that the line is not so thick that the values are obscured. If the values are to be read from the top of the emboldened line, rather than the middle, this should be clear.

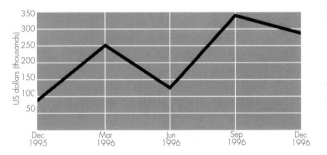

Using a tint of black or colour with the grid lines reversed to read white gives a solid feel to the whole image. The graph line can be printed in black or colour to contrast.

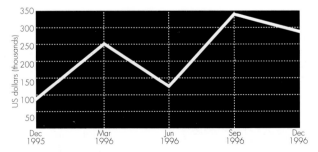

A black background with white graph line is even stronger. A dotted line is used to 'knock back' the grid.

## 3-D AND OTHER ENHANCEMENTS

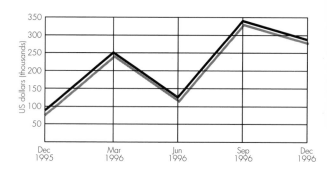

Add 3-D strengthening to the graph with a 'dropped shadow', plotted by sliding the base tracing down and to the right after drawing the graph line. It is drawn on an overlay to print grey or colour. (Don't draw the shadow where it is overlapped by the graph line.)

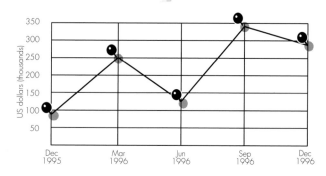

Use a drawn map pin as a graphic device to draw attention to the data points.

The pin head is constructed from two dry-transfer circles, one large black, for the complete head, and a smaller white one for the highlight. An angled line, representing the pin, connects this to the datum point. The shadow is drawn as a

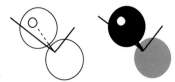

circle the same size as the pin head, but on an overlay and then printed in a tint of black or colour. Use colour for the map pins too, in order to brighten the chart.

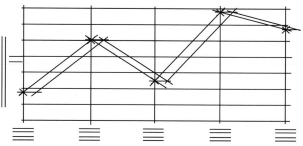

A 3-D graph line on a grid works well, providing the 'data picture' does not conflict and as long as the effect does not obscure the legibility of the graph. Plot as a simple graph but before inking, drag the trace down and to the right or the left, keeping the axes parallel. An angle of 30°, 45°, 60° or 180° is usual.

Ink in the front 'edge' of the graph line first. Add the angled lines that join the front and back edge, then the grid lines, but not across the 3-D graph line. Add shading to any underside that shows and use a thick line to emphasize the front edge .

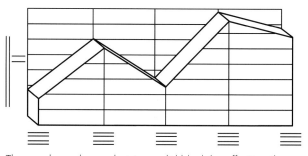

The graph can be made into a solid block by offsetting the grid lines and drawing them to appear on the front of the graph block.

## GETTING GRAPHS IN PERSPECTIVE

Based on the method described on pages 16 and 17, line
graphs can be plotted in a perspective projection. The choice
of viewpoint (above, below or from left- or righthand side) will
determine the effect. Plotting a chart viewed from above or
below is quite complex and should only be used with simple
charts. Always plot the graph in a basic flat form first in order
to visualize what effect the perspective projection will have.

### The side view

The side view is easier to
plot than the end view. This
first example shows the
graph viewed with the
righthand edge in the
foreground. This gives
emphasis to the most recent
data. Increasing the degree
of perspective by making
the lefthand edge even
shallower will exaggerate
the illusion of depth.
It is important to include a
grid in a perspective plot
so that the viewer can read
off the values.

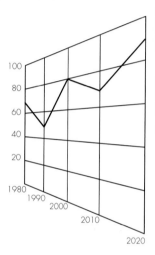

### The end view

This example foreshortens the depth of the graph so that the
graph line is more prominent and the higher values
featured. When viewed from below the graph line variations
are diminished. Although based on the same data set as the
chart above this graph takes up less vertical space. The
apparent depth is an optical illusion created by the
perspective plot.

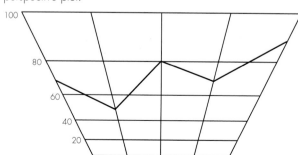

## Plotting the side view

Draw a grid with vertical and horizontal divisions. To plot the data points you can either plot them all on the front (longest) and back verticals and transfer each to its grid line, or you can treat each vertical grid line separately and calculate the conversion factor for each point.

A diminishing thickness of line enhances the perspective effect. Choose a suitable thickness for the line at the front edge of the chart of, say, one unit. When calculating the point position 310, for example, also calculate the position for 309, with 225 plot 224, and so on. Mark both these values on the plot.

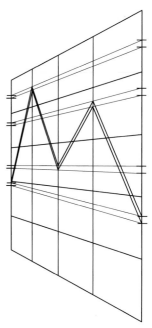

## Plotting the end view

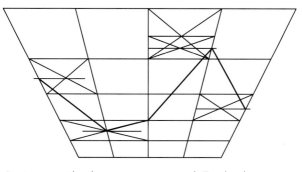

Again start with a basic perspective grid. To plot datum points use the same intersecting diagonal method to sub-divide the vertical scale until the closest possible value to the desired datum value is reached and the point can be drawn accurately or by eye. This process can become quite complex, particularly when great precision is required. Alternatively a grid can be drawn on logarithmic graph paper. Although easier to use, this does not create such a convincing perspective effect.

## LINE GRAPHS AND AWKWARD DATA

Life would be a great joy if all the data we were asked to turn into charts was as a well-behaved as that used in the examples so far. However, life is not that simple and so here are a few suggestions for dealing with unruly data.

### Vast differences in values

Because the line graph is designed to show the variations between values by drawing a line from one to another this is not usually a problem. However there are times when the subtle differences between some values which are close together are more important than the greater, more obvious ones.

20   590  600  595  605  15

This data set has a substantial rise at one end and dramatic fall at the other. If this is plotted on a straightforward graph the differences at the higher levels are not clearly seen.
(A similar problem would arise if only one datum were high and the others all low.)

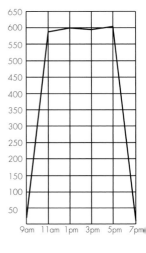

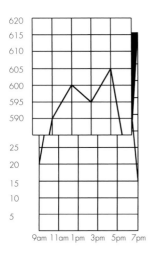

One simple way to highlight the upper values is by plotting the graph in two parts. This allows the upper range to be magnified sufficiently to show the variations while still indicating the greater differences. A graphic device, such as 'folding', helps the reader understand that these are two sections of a single chart.

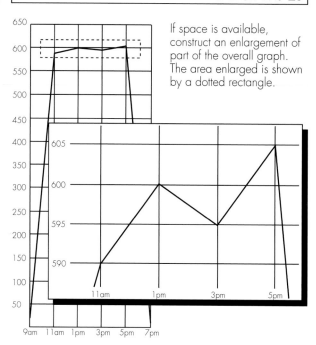

If space is available, construct an enlargement of part of the overall graph. The area enlarged is shown by a dotted rectangle.

## Estimated and projected values

Quite often a data set will include one or more values, usually the last one in the series, which have been estimated or projected. Usually an asterisk or superscript number with a

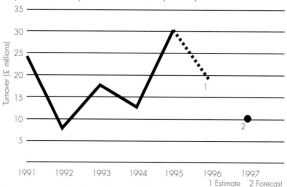

footnote to mark the value is all that is needed.
If it is necessary to draw particular attention to estimated or projected data, use a screened or dotted line. A datum point could even be drawn as an isolated point by not extending the graph line to its position.

**Negative values**
Combining negative and positive values on one chart presents no problem as the zero line on the Y-axis can be positioned at any sensible, convenient level. Use a tinted or dotted line to stress the negative portion. If the graph is in colour use a different colour for the negative values on the axis.

The negative aspect can be stressed by using a colour for the whole area below the line and reversing out the graph line to read white.

● When plotting a graph that includes positive and negative values remember to add both together for the purpose of calculating the depths. In this example the total depth of the grid is 100 units.

Omitting the grid below the zero line gives a dramatic effect with the graph line appearing to fall off the bottom of the chart. In the absence of a labelled axis include the data as labels.

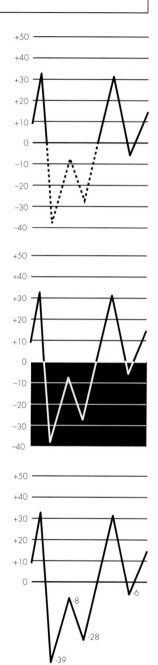

## ALTERNATIVE PRESENTATIONS

Conventionally a graph is presented as a straightforward 'picture' of the comparative data. However, there may be reasons for devising an alternative treatment, either because space restricts the conventional view, or because the information to be shown on the graph has a particular pattern.

## The horizontal graph

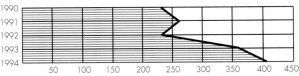

The line graph can be effective in a horizontal format. The chart is constructed in the same way as a vertical graph, but with the axes transposed. It is effective when trying to emphasize value differences in a confined vertical space.

## The circular graph

This has a particular application in showing a repeating cycle, so that the line is continuous. The grid is made up of a series of concentric circles. The total cycle is divided by radii at regular intervals, so that a twelve monthly cycle has radii at $360° \div 12 = 30°$ intervals.

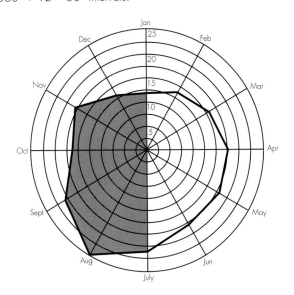

Tone or colour can be used to pick out particular segments.

## MULTIPLE GRAPHS
Certain kinds of data require a more detailed and complex
approach than the basic line graph. Sometimes alternative
scale measurements are required for one graph line. Multiple
graphs allow you to combine two or more graph lines on a
single chart. These options require careful planning to
maintain the important principle of any chart or diagram —
clearly presented information with immediate graphic impact.

## Dual scales
While not exactly a multiple graph, the dual scale with a
single graph line occurs, for example, when comparing metric
values with imperial values. Show one scale on either side of
the graph if possible and use different line styles for the scales.

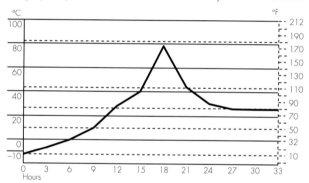

## Dual line graph
When colour is available use a different colour for each line
to make sure each is clearly distinguishable. When working in
black and white use different line styles or break one line
either side of the other at the crossover point.

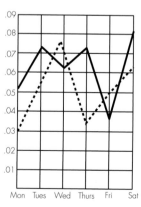
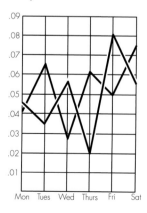

## Multiple graph lines

The same guidance applies when there are more than two lines. Make sure each is distinguishable from the others.

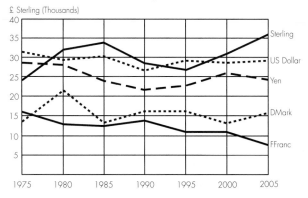

As labelling can be problematical with a cluster of lines, try to use a key, or label the lines at the edge of the graph.
If there are not too many crossovers, or if the lines are conveniently separate, line styles (or tones or colours) may be duplicated.

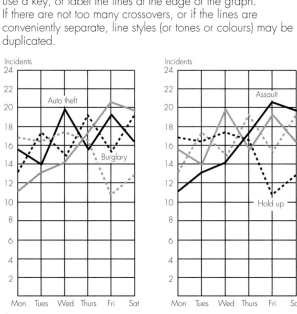

If the lines are impossibly clustered use two, or more, graphs highlighting just a few lines on each but showing the others 'ghosted' in a light grey line so that the comparison can be made. These graphs should appear as close as possible to each other so that they can easily be assimilated.

## Area, stacked or accumulative graphs

These are multiple graphs with the topmost line showing a total value and the other lines representing subdivisions. This style of chart can only convey a general picture of the subsections, as only the lowest subsection line and the total line relate directly to the scale shown on the Y-axis.

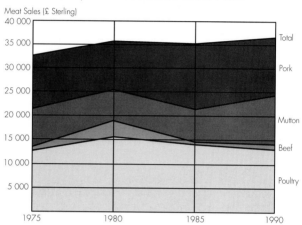

Meat Sales (£ Sterling)

Annotation can be a problem, particularly when bands are too narrow to accommodate a label. Try to position labels so that they align vertically with each other and keep them horizontal. This helps to locate the relevant information. If there is insufficient space within the chart place labels at the edge of the graph.

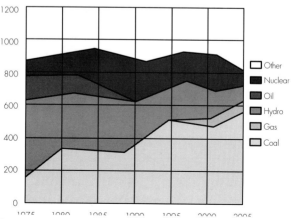

If some categories do not extend across the whole graph use a key to identify subsections.

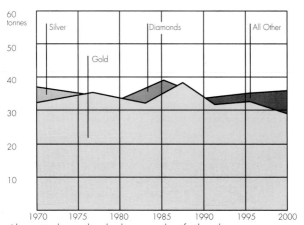

Alternatively use leader lines to identify the elements.

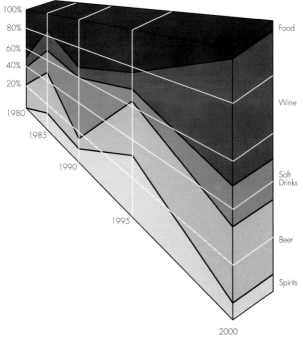

This example shows a stacked graph in perspective with a constant total value of 100%, so the top line remains level, whereas the others indicate the breakdown of that total. Note that grid lines are drawn on the face and on the top surface.

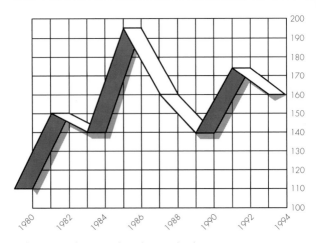

*Above* 3-D line graph with cast shadow.
*Below left* 3-D area graph.
*Below right* Multiple graph.

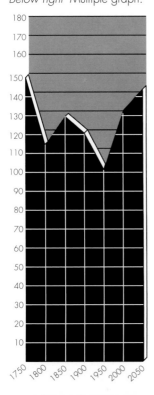

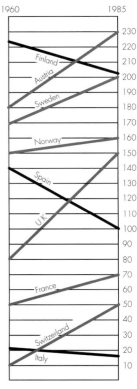

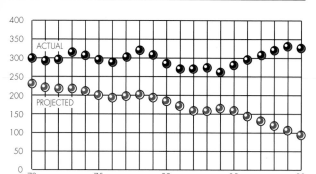

*Above* Double line graph using symbols, omitting actual graph line and showing points only.

*Below* Mirrored 3-D horizontal graph.

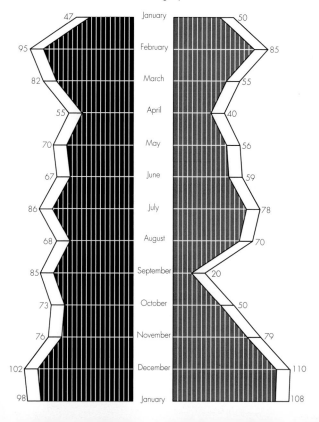

# BAR CHARTS

## CONSTRUCTING A BAR CHART

The basic bar chart usually consists of two or more bars, the lengths of which represent comparative values of data. The bars can be horizontal, vertical or angled, but are usually parallel.

A brief might appear as follows:
River Thames  218 miles; Rhine   830 miles;
R Rhône  811 km;  Hudson River  350 miles;
Loire  625 miles.

Before commencing the plot take a little time to organize the data. This can save a lot of reworking time later.
● Sort the data into consistent units (the Rhône data has been given in kilometres but all the others in miles). Use a conversion table to recalculate if necessary.
● Put the data in a sensible order. This could be in alphabetical order of river name, in ascending or descending order of the lengths, or be determined by other factors.
● Make sure label copy is consistent. Should 'river' be spelt out in full or be abbreviated? Should it have a capital 'R'? Does the abbreviation appear before or after the name?
● Have the commissioning client approve the terminology, confirm any recalculation and approve the order.
● Choose a suitable typeface and size for labels.

| | |
|---|---|
| R.Rhine | 830 miles |
| R.Loire | 625 miles |
| R.Rhône | 507 miles |
| R.Hudson | 350 miles |
| R.Thames | 218 miles |

Once the data is in order you can plan the chart. To obtain the optimum comparison between the bar lengths, and as rivers typically flow horizontally, a horizontal bar chart seems a good idea, so the chart is schemed across the page width. Remember to allow room at either end of the bars for label copy, using a type cast-off of the longest label. Be sure to leave some space between the label and the bar.

R HUDSON

**62mm**
**Space available**
**for longest bar**

830 mi

The drawing area remaining is 62mm and this represents the value of the longest river/bar - 830 miles. Now the other river/bar lengths can be calculated in proportion.

## Proportioning with a calculator

Key the bar length of 62 (mm) into the calculator and divide it by the river length 830 (miles). This gives an answer of .0746987 and this is the conversion factor for the other values. Round it down to three decimal places –.075 – which is accurate enough (see below). Jot down the chosen factor on the reference data sheet and enter it into the (cleared) memory (M+) on the calculator. Make sure it is the only value in the memory by pressing the memory read key (MR or equivalent). Multiply each of the other river length values by this factor to obtain the bar lengths in millimetres and write these against the actual values on the reference.

The table shows the comparative bar lengths with the conversion factor at two (a), three (b) and seven (c) decimal places. The values in columns (b) and (c) hardly vary at all whereas the top value in column (a) is over 4mm shorter, 7% out. (The converted values have been rounded to one decimal place as the thickness of a fine drawing pen is not much bigger than .1mm.). Clearly, in a chart this size a conversion factor at three decimal places has optimum accuracy

| | **a** | **b** | **c** |
|---|---|---|---|
| miles | .07 | .075 | .0746987 |
| 830 | 58.1mm | 62.2mm | 62.0mm |
| 625 | 43.7 | 46.9 | 46.7 |
| 507 | 35.5 | 38.0 | 37.9 |
| 350 | 24.5 | 26.2 | 26.1 |
| 218 | 15.3 | 16.3 | 16.3 |

Now that the values have been calculated the bar lengths can be plotted from the left hand 'baseline' on the trace.

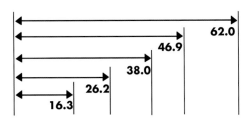

The width of the bars is now determined. If space is no problem then an aesthetically pleasing, easy to calculate depth can be chosen.

If, however, the available total depth is pre-determined, the bars will need to be sized to fit. Allow for any annotation that is to appear above or below the chart within the available space. Given a remaining total depth of 26.5mm, for example, divide that by five to get the bar depths (5.3mm) and mark the divisions on the trace. Alternatively use one of the methods described on pages 14 and 15 to divide the total depth into five equal units. Check that the bars are a consistent width by marking off the width of one on the edge of a piece of paper and then sliding this down over all the others to discover any discrepancies, which should be corrected at this stage.

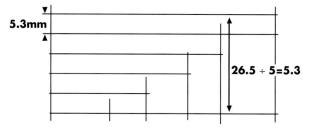

**5.3mm**

**26.5 ÷ 5=5.3**

The bars can now be drawn in position on the base tracing and, if the design is acceptable, the chart can be inked in.

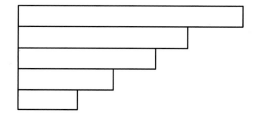

## Adding labels

Now the annotation is added to the chart at the specified type size. By ranging left the river names and vertically centring them on each bar and by placing the values evenly spaced from the end of each bar we have a neatly labelled and clear diagram. Don't forget to include any heading.

COMPARATIVE RIVER LENGTHS

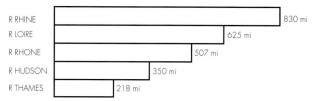

R RHINE    830 mi
R LOIRE    625 mi
R RHONE    507 mi
R HUDSON    350 mi
R THAMES    218 mi

## VARIATIONS ON A THEME

Before creating final artwork the chart can be modified to
increase its usefulness or make its appearance more
interesting. But before launching on any elaborate design, plot
the chart in its simple, basic form to aid planning.

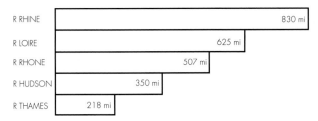

In this first example the longest bar has been extended to the
right hand margin and the other lengthened in proportion.The
data labels are placed within the bars. This emphasizes the
variations in length. (Instead of recalculating the lengths use a
photocopier or enlarger to extend the bars to the new length.)

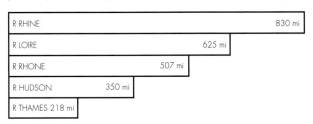

Using the same method the diagram can be extended to the
full column width. In the available width this gives the best
comparison of the river lengths.

Keeping the bar lengths as they were originally but making
them thinner and filled with black or a colour strengthens the
chart. With just a few bars this is quite striking but could be
visually jarring if there were many bars. A patterned fill could
also be used, but avoid making the diagram too 'busy'.

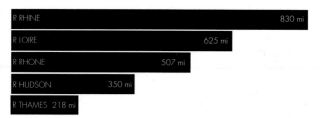

Reversing out type to read white on full width black bars adds even more emphasis.

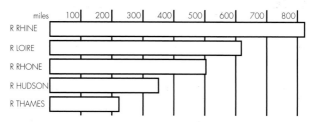

The next variation leaves off the exact value (although these could have been included) and gives a more generalized picture by using a scaled grid (see page 42 ).

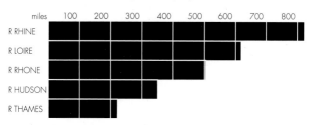

Still keeping the grid but reversing this out of solid black bars makes it easier to 'read off' the values.

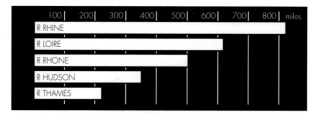

Create a more regular overall shape by reversing the chart out of a black or colour background.

## Constructing a grid

A background grid serves as a ruler to help the reader compare differences in bar lengths and can be used instead of labelling values on bars. Plotting the grid is a simple extension of the method used to create the bars.

Decide whether you want the longest bar to fill the available space and make the grid fit to the nearest grid line short of the full length, or the grid to fit the space and reduce the bars to fit that. Three options are shown below.

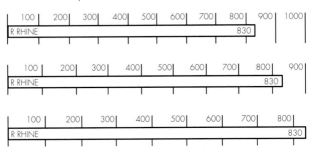

Deciding the grid style can be both an editorial and an aesthetic choice. An identical grid could be used for a group of charts, or each grid could be determined by the length of the longest bar on the individual chart. Be sure to establish the style before plotting all the charts.

Grid lines should be at regular intervals - such as every ten units, or every twenty-five units etc. It is also usual to end the grid on a full division, so a grid might be 200 units long with lines at every ten units, or one thousand units long with divisions at 100 units. Ending the grid at the interval below the longest bar, as in the river examples, gives emphasis to the longest bar and allows all the bars to be of optimum length. Don't use too many divisions as this will clutter the chart and may not leave enough space to fit the labels.

Subdivisions along the grid can be left unlabelled as long as each label clearly relates to its own line.

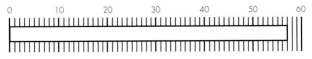

The bar can be divided into sections to simulate a grid.

## THE VERTICAL BAR CHART

Although the choice between vertical and horizontal chart can be purely a matter of preference, there are times when the vertical chart is more appropriate. In western culture we are accustomed to reading from left to right, so any chronological progression is expected to read in that way and time data generally appears along the X-axis.

The vertical bar chart is usually constructed to rise from a common base line. This line should represent zero. If it does not it should be clearly labelled. The bars should be as long as possible within the available space in order to demonstrate comparative values.

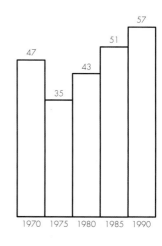

## Fitting labels in tight spaces

In some cases fitting labels on a vertical bar chart can be problematical, particularly when the bars are very narrow.
Labels can be run vertically, though this makes them difficult to read.

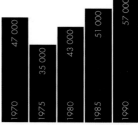

Running the labels at an angle makes the data more legible. Keep the angle and direction consistent. Slanting up from left up to right is easier to read than slanting down.

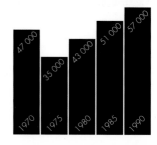

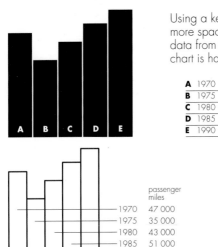

Using a key table takes up more space and separates data from the bars, so the chart is harder to assimilate.

| | | |
|---|---|---|
| **A** | 1970 | 47 000 passenger miles |
| **B** | 1975 | 35 000 |
| **C** | 1980 | 43 000 |
| **D** | 1985 | 51 000 |
| **E** | 1990 | 57 000 |

You can combine the table and diagram by using 'leader' lines to connect each label to its bar.

|  | passenger miles |
|---|---|
| 1970 | 47 000 |
| 1975 | 35 000 |
| 1980 | 43 000 |
| 1985 | 51 000 |
| 1990 | 57 000 |

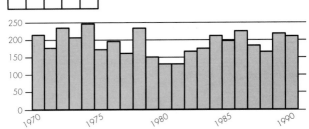

Where there are a a large number of bars use a grid to show the values. If the bars are in a sequence label every other bar, or every fifth bar, for example.

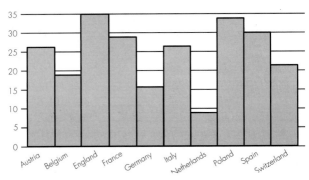

If each individual bar needs identification use slanted type below the bar.

## GRAPHIC ENHANCEMENTS

There is an almost unlimited number of variations and combinations of variations which can add interest to a diagram without losing the information.

Use a 'drop shadow' to lift a chart off the page. Create the shadow effect by sliding the base tracing down and across. After drawing the additional lines fill the shadow area with black, or a tint or colour. There are no rules for position of shadow but a 45° angle will give equal width of shadow to the side and below. Don't make the shadow too thin.

Leaving space between bars takes up more overall depth. Shadows can also be raised, rather than dropped, but work better when seen on two sides rather than just one.

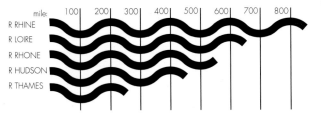

It is sometimes possible to employ a graphic device that relates to the subject matter – wavy lines to represent rivers, railway tracks or roads for travel, and so on. Bear in mind the context in which the chart will appear and don't be too frivolous. Be careful not to create something you can't easily draw – constructing parallel curves requires drafting skill.

## 3-D AND PERSPECTIVE BAR CHARTS

3-D and perspective projections add solidity to the bar chart and are not difficult as long as basic rules are followed.

### Simple simulation

The simplest way to create a 3-D effect is by adding a slanted top and end to the bar. The bars should be made shorter, but in proportion to each other, to allow for the ends within the available width. Use any angle, but set-squares make 30°, 45° or 60° easiest to construct.

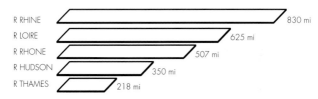

Plot the bars as previously shown but draw the bar ends at an angle and use a heavier line on the front and the revealed ends (in this case the righthand ends).

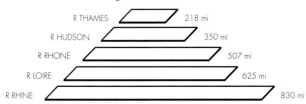

If the bars are aligned with the angle of the ends a pyramid effect is achieved. This obviously works best when the bars are arranged in ascending or descending order.

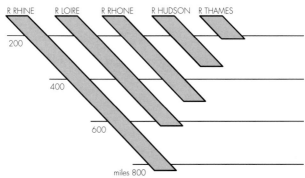

A vertical bar chart can be treated in a similar way by slanting the sides and leaving the ends horizontal.

## 3-D PROJECTION

Technical drawing projections (axonometric, oblique and isometric) are used to create more advanced 3-D effects. Bars are constructed in much the same way as for a flat bar chart but sides and ends are projected from the basic structure. As associated lines are drawn parallel the bar lengths can be measured against a ruler, whereas true perspective 3-D has converging lines and cannot be properly measured.

**Oblique** projections have one face parallel to the picture plane, the other faces angled from that. Any angle is acceptable, but for the convenience of a set-square choose 30°, 45° or 60°.

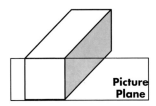

**Axonometric** projections have all planes angled to the picture plane. The angles for the left and right faces can be different as long as they are consistent for each face.

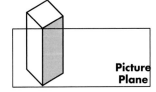

**Isometric** projections are axonometric projections with the same angle for the left and right face. 30° or 45° are most common, but any other angle may be used.

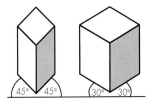

## Oblique angled horizontal bar chart

This the simplest of the projections to draw. Add an angled top and end to the basic bar.

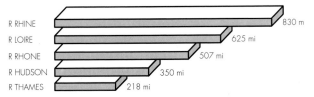

| | |
|---|---|
| R RHINE | 830 m |
| R LOIRE | 625 mi |
| R RHONE | 507 mi |
| R HUDSON | 350 mi |
| R THAMES | 218 mi |

The bars can be overlapped to keep the chart compact.

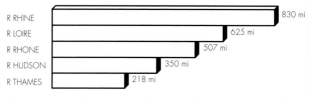

Alternatively the bars can be drawn to abut each other with the tops and ends drawn only where visible.

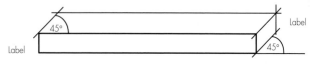

● Remember to allow space to fit any labels at the ends of the bars and for the depth of the tops of the bars. Make sure that the angle used is consistent.

## Oblique angled vertical bar chart
Although basically a vertical chart this type of diagram appears to project horizontally towards or away from the viewer. Choosing the angle and direction of projection is important as this determines the length of the bars and the degree of contrast between them.

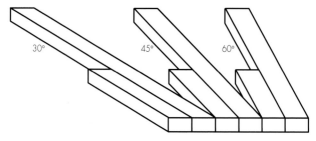

If the bars project back at an acute angle from a foreground baseline and so that the longest bar is angled across as much of the width as possible, the optimum contrast is achieved. As the angle is made less acute the degree of contrast is reduced. The acutely angled bar is also more difficult to label and requires a narrower bar width than the others.

Factors such as number of bars and their relative values affect the possible projection so it needs careful planning. Draw it as a basic flat chart first to get an idea of how it might look. The bars can be arranged side by side, horizontally, or vertically, one on top of the other. The direction of the angle is also a matter of preference and can be above or below the base.

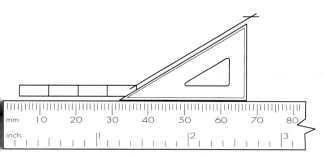

Allow space for any labelling above and below the bars, then draw a rectangle around the area available for the bars. Measure and draw the rectangles for the bases of the bars starting from the appropriate corner. Plot the edge of the longest bar within the available space at the chosen angle, marking the endpoint.

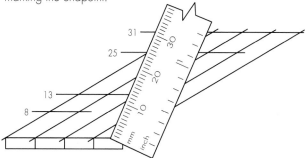

Draw the top edges of the remaining bars parallel to the longest bar. Measure and mark the bar lengths. If the data do not correspond directly to ruler measurements, angle the ruler to obtain a suitable conversion measurement (see page 14).

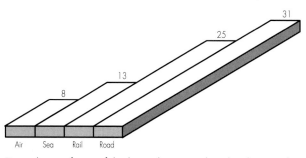

Draw the top faces of the bars, then complete the diagram by drawing in the visible portions of the sides of the bars. Adding a tint to the sides and bases helps emphasize the 3-D effect.

## Isometric bar chart

Like the oblique projection, the isometric projection is
measurable with a ruler, which makes it relatively
straightforward to construct. The instructions below describe
how to plot a vertical bar chart, but can be applied to the
horizontal bar chart.

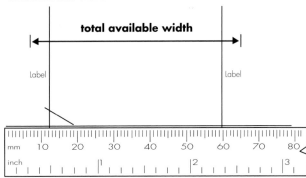

Leave space for labelling and draw vertical lines for the left-
and righthand edges of the bar chart. The leftmost vertical line
determines the position of the corner of the leftmost bar.
Draw a horizontal rule about 20mm below the chart area
extending either side of the diagram and hold the ruler in
place along this line. With a set-square held against the
straight edge, draw a line at 30° down to the right, cutting
the left vertical and extending towards the ruler.

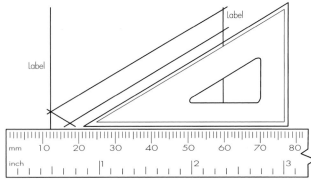

Decide how 'thick' you want the bars, and, keeping the
straight edge firmly in position, rotate the set-square and draw
the 30° angled front and back lines to form the base. Still
keeping the ruler in position rotate the set-square again and
draw a line through the point where the front base line cuts
the righthand vertical.

Having established the base of the bars, measure the front baseline and divide this by the number of bars to establish the bar width.

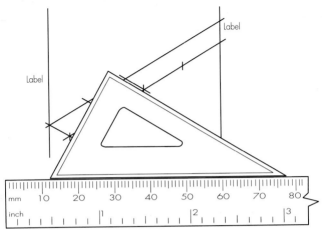

Mark these off against the edge of the ruler then, placing the straightedge along the lower horizontal, draw the angled lines to form the bases of the individual bars.
Keep the ruler in place and draw vertical lines from the corners of the base shapes to form the sides of the bars, sliding the set-square along the straightedge. It is important to keep the ruler firmly in position in order to keep lines parallel.

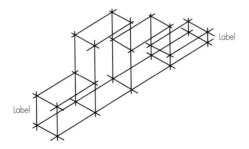

Select the righthand back vertical of the longest bar and measure up from the back baseline to mark the height (allowing room for labels). Use this to calculate the other bar lengths, measuring these along the vertical sides at the back. Holding the ruler on the base horizontal guide add the other bar tops to complete the plot.

## TUBULAR BARS

3-D bars need not be rectangular in section but can be drawn as cylinders, using an ellipse or circle for the ends of the bars. The ellipse angle (stated on the ellipse template) determines how circular the ellipse is, a circle being a 90° ellipse. If plotting a cylindrical chart in isometric use the special ellipse which is set at 35° 16'. The depth of the ellipse is determined by the fixed widths of the diameters on the template.

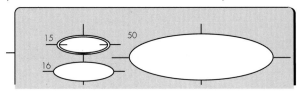

In the allocated space draw a baseline for the bars. Place the template so that the bottom of the ellipse touches the baseline and, making sure the widest diameter of the ellipse (the major axis) is parallel to the base, draw the ellipse. Also plot the aligning marks of the major axis onto the trace.

Draw a horizontal centre line through the aligning marks on the trace to extend beyond the edges of the chart area.

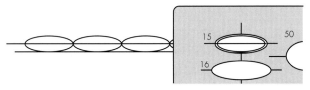

Now draw the base ellipses for the other bars using the centre line to align the ellipses.

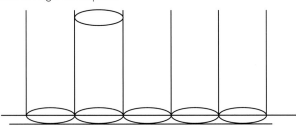

Draw the vertical side lines for the cylinders, making sure they are parallel. Draw the top of the longest bar so that the top of the ellipse touches the top of the chart area (allow for labels).

Measure the height of the longest bar, from top of ellipse to top of ellipse, or from base to base. Use this measurement to calculate the proportionate lengths of the other bars.

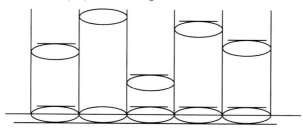

Plot the heights of the bars. Be sure to work only from top to top or from base to base of each ellipse.

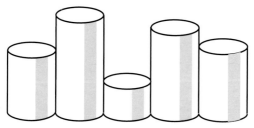

Finish the chart by inking in the bars, drawing only the lower half of the baseline ellipses, and adding labels.

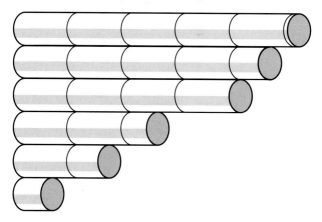

Horizontal cylindrical bar charts are drawn following the same process. Adding more ellipses or circles at measured intervals creates a form of grid. The grid intervals are calculated from the length of the longest bar.

## BAR CHARTS IN PERSPECTIVE

Perspective bar charts require careful construction as the values cannot always be measured with a ruler. They are drawn in either one-point perspective or two-point perspective. Parallel lines are plotted to converge on vanishing points drawn on a horizon line. In one-point perspective a second point is set at infinity, so all the lines drawn to that point are drawn as parallel. Charts can be viewed end-on or face-on but the end-on view foreshortens the bar and exaggerates or reduces the perceived differences between values. Dramatic effects can be created using perspective but beware of distorting the information.

### One point perspective – values undistorted

This is a basic bar chart with 3-D perspective sides and ends.

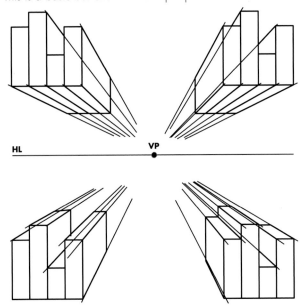

The relationship to the horizon line (HL) and the vanishing point (VP) determines the effect, so the chart can be seen from above, below or either side. The depth of the bars is a matter of preference.

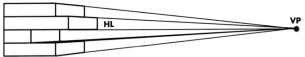

The bar chart can be horizontal or vertical.

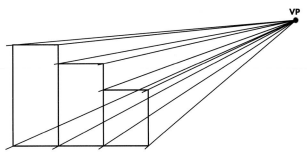

First establish the desired position of the vanishing point in relation to the chart, then plot the front faces of the bars. Draw lines from the bar ends to the vanishing point.

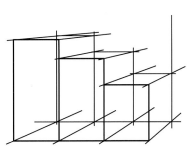

Draw a line parallel to the edge of the righthand bar to represent the thickness of that bar. Where this line cuts the line from the bottom corner to the vanishing point draw another line parallel to the base. Then draw lines up from the point at which the depth line cuts the lines projected back to the vanishing point until they meet the perspective lines at the tops of the bars.

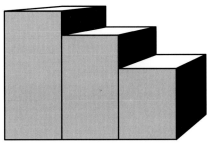

The plotted chart can now be finished, drawing in any ends that are exposed. Note that the sides of the bars in the final chart reduce in apparent thickness as they approach the vanishing point.

## One point perspective – values distorted

Constructing a bar chart so that it recedes towards the vanishing point distorts the relativity of the bars. The charts below are all based on the same data set

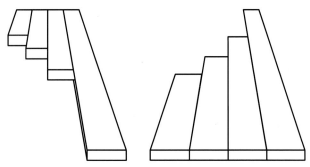

In a chart viewed end-on with the baseline in the foreground the relative differences diminish whereas they are exaggerated if the baseline is drawn near the horizon line.

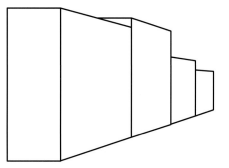

When a chart is drawn side-on bar heights will diminish proportionately towards the vanishing point.

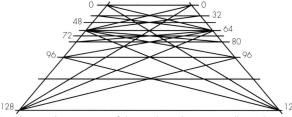

To draw either version of the end-on chart you will need to construct a perspective grid (see pages 16 and 17). This grid will need to be detailed enough to enable the bar lengths to be plotted as accurately as possible.

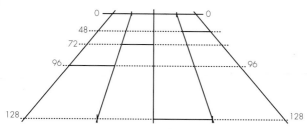

Mark the foreground line (whether chart baseline or top) with the bar widths and draw the faces of the bars to length.

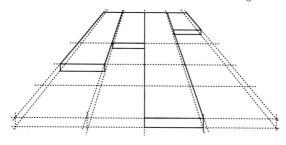

Draw the bar ends as a series of rectangles.

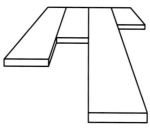

Ink in the faces of the bars and those parts of the ends and sides that are visible (some lines may be obscured).

To construct a chart viewed from the side, first draw the horizon line and mark the vanishing point. Draw a vertical line at the foreground front edge of the nearest bar. This can be above, below or through the horizon line.
Plot the base point of the first bar and all the bar heights on the vertical line.

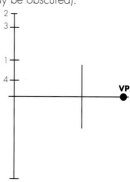

Draw lines from the topmost mark and from the base mark to the vanishing point. Now construct a perspective grid in order to plot the bar widths. This will entail simple sub-division for groups of 4, 8 or 16 bars etc. but for other groups you will need to extend the grid as described on page 17.

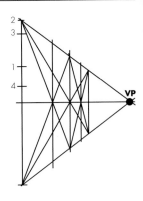

Align a ruler with the vanishing point and each of the bar heights in turn and transfer these to their relative bars.
Choose a suitable width for the foremost bar and draw in the side, the top and bottom lines being parallel to the horizon line. Then draw a line from the lefthand edge of the base of this bar to the vanishing point. This is the back baseline.

Draw horizontal lines for the base of the side of each bar and where these cut the back baseline plot a vertical line for each bar that has an exposed portion of the side. Ink in the exposed lines to complete the chart.

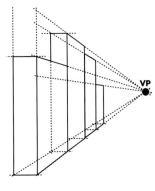

## Two point perspective – values distorted

This type of chart is schemed in a similar way to the previous one but has a second vanishing point. This gives additional emphasis to the foreground bar. Constructing the chart is quite complex and it is not recommended if there are many bars. In two-point perspective values are always distorted. The distortion increases as the vanishing points are moved closer.

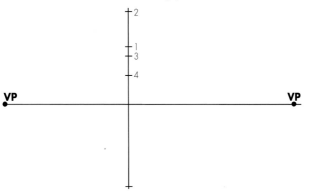

Establish the two vanishing points along the horizon line in relation to the proposed bar positions. Draw the foremost vertical of the front bar and mark off the heights of all the other bars along this line. Identify each value clearly to avoid confusion. Any values greater than that of the foremost bar should be plotted in relative position.

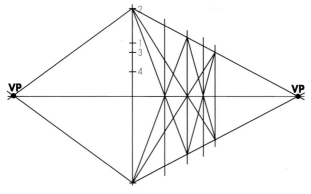

Draw a line from the topmost value and from the base mark to both vanishing points. Decide how wide the combined bars will be along the front face. Using the method for drawing a perspective grid by intersecting diagonals described on pages 16–17, construct the correct number of bar divisions.

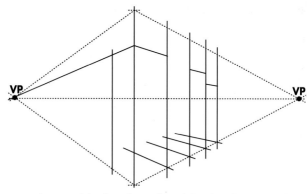

Draw the top of the front face of each bar by aligning a ruler with the vanishing point and the appropriate mark on the foremost vertical. Now draw lines from the bases of all bars to the other vanishing point.

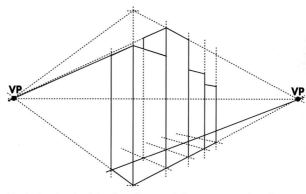

Mark the depth of the front bar and draw a vertical so that it cuts the lines to the vanishing points. From the point where this

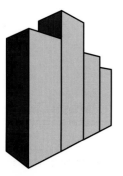

cuts the lower lefthand line draw the back baseline to the other vanishing point. Draw exposed sides by drawing verticals up from the base corner points of each bar.

Use shading to emphasize the 3-D structure.

## COPING WITH AWKWARD DATA

Here are ways of dealing with a few of the most common
problems encountered in constructing bar charts.

**Irregular time periods** within an otherwise regular time
scale (most frequently the last entry) need to be highlighted.
There are two variations of this.
1. A period between datum points is irregular:

1960;   1970;   1980;   1985

2. One point covers a greater or lesser period than the others:

1960–70      1970–80      1980–90      1990–95

In either case an asterisk or number with a footnote may be
enough but a visual indication is much clearer. The same
treatment may be used for either.

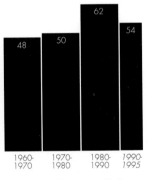

Using a different width for
the exceptional bar draws
attention and indicates that it
is a reduced period.

Or you can highlight the bar
with a different tone or
colour and use a different
typographic treatment for the
labelling.

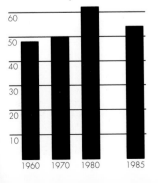

This third method leaves the
bar the same width as the
others but isolates it from the
main group so that it is
perceived as being different.

**Big differences in values** can occur within sets of data.

| March | April | May | June |
|-------|-------|-----|------|
| 370   | 390   | 330 | 4200 |

Given data which are all close in value except for the last number, which is nearly eleven times bigger than the highest of the others, a basic chart would not show the differences between the smaller values.
The first solution simply shows a reduction in the longest bar length with a clear indication that the bar has been broken or cut.

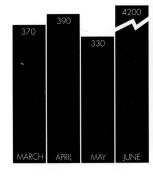

A graphic variation shows the bar folded indicating the break.
If the difference is not too great, the bar could be drawn with more folds so that it would appear that if unfolded the length of the bar would be in proportion to the lengths of the other bars.

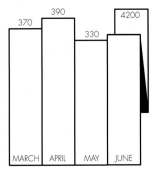

An arrow head on the top of the abbreviated bar indicates that the bar should be perceived as extending beyond the vertical scale of the drawn chart.

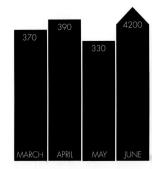

**All values are large** and so the differences do not show up on a regular chart.

5260    5460    5320    5370    5260

The solution is to have the base of the chart set not at zero but at a suitable higher value so that the range on the chart is much narrower.

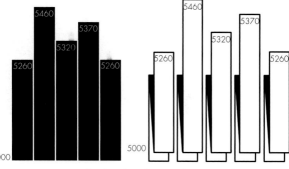

It is important to make the chart base value quite clear to the reader. Use folded bars to indicate this graphically.

**Estimated and projected values** are often included in data, particularly in financial reports. Indicating that these are projected or estimated values is important. Again a footnote may be adequate but a visual highlight is clearer, drawing the reader's attention immediately to the point .

| 1980 | 1985 | 1990 | 1995 |
|------|------|------|------|
| 24.5 | 22.7 | 33.4 | 47.2 (estimated) |

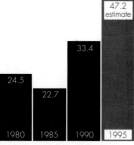

Identify the estimated figure by making the last bar a different tone or colour.

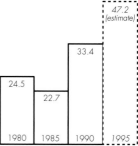

Italicize the value label and draw the bar with a dotted line to stress the unfinalized structure.

**Negative values** can be a particular problem as the bar chart is usually constructed from a baseline set at zero.

| UK | USA | USSR | GDR | Other |
|----|-----|------|-----|-------|
| 45 | 64  | 75   | −32 | 48    |

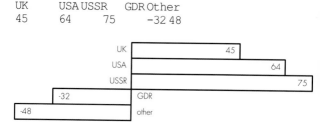

Plotting the bars either side of a zero base line requires sufficient space for the longest positive value and the longest negative value. This reduces the differentiation between the other positive values.

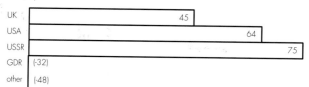

The simplest solution, if it is acceptable editorially, is to omit negative bars and just show their value in brackets.

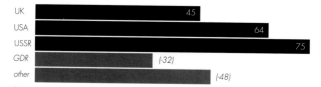

One or other of the highlighting or ghosting devices could be employed.

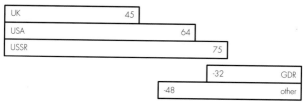

A third option is to use two overlapping charts, one with positive values running from left to right, and the other showing the negative values constructed from a separate baseline and running right to left.

## THE SPLIT OR DIVIDED BAR CHART

Before moving on to deal with combined or multiple bar charts there is a variation of the basic bar chart which needs explanation. The split, or divided, bar chart is included here as it is only rarely used in its single form, appearing most frequently as a multiple chart.

In its simple form it consists of a single bar, representing a total value, which is sub-divided into segments. The value of the total may be labelled or left to the reader to calculate.

| | |
|---|---|
| 0.6 | ALBANIA |
| 0.8 | BULGARIA |
| 0.7 | CZECHOSLOVAKIA |
| 0.4 | EAST GERMANY |
| 0.5 | HUNGARY |
| 0.3 | POLAND |
| 0.5 | ROMANIA |

The most common problem encountered with the single split bar is in clearly showing and labelling small segments. This can be solved in the flat bar by slightly exaggerating minute sections and using leader lines to indicate labels.

London
Manchester
Birmingham
Liverpool
Glasgow
Newcastle
Southhampton
Cardiff

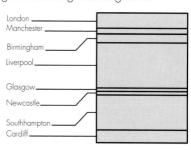

United Kingdom 42%
France 2%
German 2%
Sweden 10%
Spain 24%
U.S.A 60%

Other 10
Oats 30
Barley 60
Maize 120
Wheat 160
Rice 320

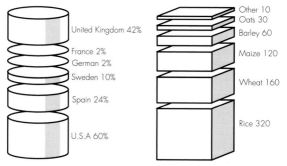

Using a three dimensional chart enables small sections to be shown as flat planes. Design the depth of the projection so that the labels will fit comfortably beside segments.

## MULTIPLE BAR CHARTS

Having established the basic principles of the bar chart this section deals with the multiple bar chart in which two or more bar charts are combined in one diagram.

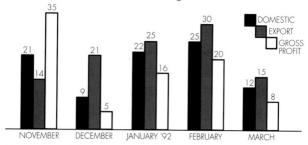

The chart could be constructed from a combination of two or more sets of data with a common axis. These may be combined as groups or clusters of bars on the same baseline.

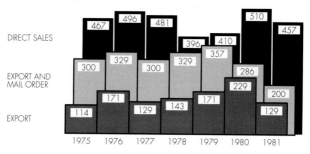

Data of this kind can also be represented as overlapping bars on the same baseline. This method only works well when the bars behind are not obscured. It is also important that the data along the X-axis clearly relate to the appropriate bars.

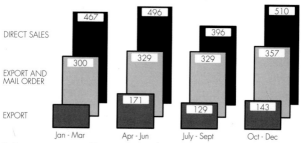

If there is space, offset each layer slightly from the baseline and separate bars so that they are seen in groups. This helps the reader to read the chart across and front to back.

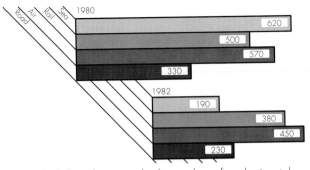

The multiple bar chart can also be made up from horizontal bar charts. Here an angled grid is used to link the axes while the bar charts appear in separate groups.

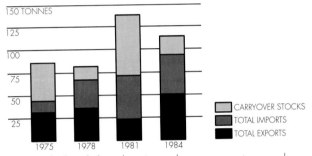

In the multiple split bar chart it may be necessary to use a key to identify segments. Plan the chart layout by adding up the values for each bar in turn in order to establish the highest total that will need to be accommodated.

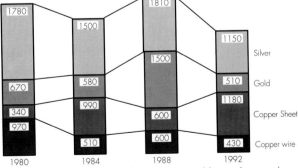

A progressive increase or decrease in total bar values and their constituent parts can be shown by drawing lines between corresponding segments on each bar. In effect this is a combined line graph and bar chart.

## The population pyramid chart

Pyramid chart, or population pyramid, is the name given to a specific format of multiple bar chart in which two sets of data are plotted either side of a common axis, appearing almost as mirror images – apart from the data variations. The name is derived from use of the chart for demographic analysis in which the Y-axis is divided by age groups with one side showing data for male and the other female.

To draw a pyramid chart you first need to establish a central axis. This is drawn as two vertical parallel lines with the common data labels between them. If the axis is to be exactly in the centre of the graphics area, deduct sufficient space from the total width to accommodate labels with space between these and the axis lines. Divide the remaining width in two and use this measurement to calculate the lengths of the bars for the chart which includes the biggest bar.

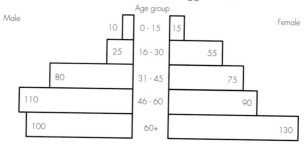

The bars for the opposite side are also plotted in exact proportion to those on the longest side.

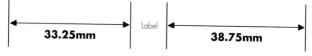

Alternatively the axis can be off-centre so that the longest bar on each side touches the edge of the area. To establish the axis position, allow space for labels and measure the width remaining within the graphics area. This is the total bar width. Add together the highest value from each side of the chart and divide the total bar width by the answer. This gives the conversion factor for all the bars. Measure the lengths of the left and right longest bars in from the outer edge of the area and draw the axis lines of the chart.

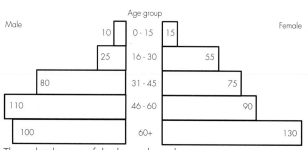

Then plot the rest of the bars along the appropriate axis.

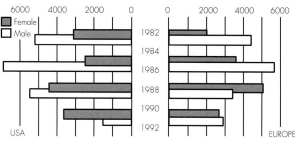

The pyramid can be made up of subdivided or 'split' bars. If the axis is centred and the longest bars are uneven a grid will help to balance the two sides.

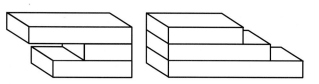

Add a 3-D edge to create an interesting effect. Note that the bars are angled in the same direction.

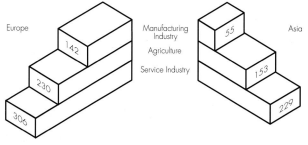

In isometric projection the bars can be angled symetrically.

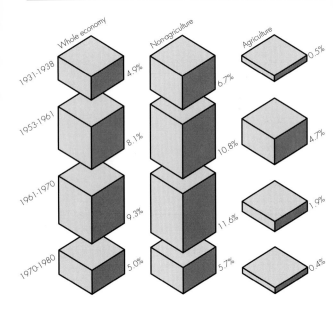

*Above* 3-D split bar chart.

*Below* Two bar multiple bar chart.

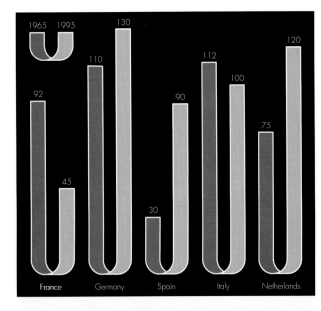

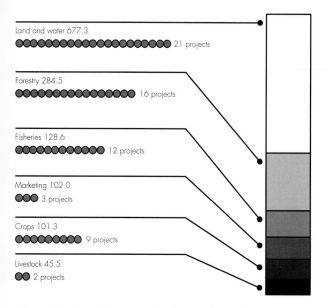

Land and water 677.3
21 projects

Forestry 284.5
16 projects

Fisheries 128.6
12 projects

Marketing 102.0
3 projects

Crops 101.3
9 projects

Livestock 45.5
2 projects

*Above* Combined horizontal and vertical bar chart using circular symbols for the horizontal bars.
*Below* Two bar multiple horizontal bar chart with grid.

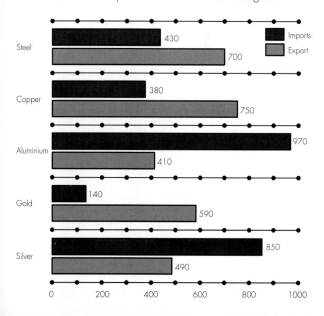

Steel
430
700

Copper
380
750

Aluminium
970
410

Gold
140
590

Silver
850
490

Imports
Export

0    200    400    600    800    1000

# AREA AND PIE CHARTS

Area charts, as the name suggests, show data comparison by comparing the total areas of a given shape. Area charts are particularly useful when comparing values with great numerical differences. The area chart is most suited to subjects related to area, such as land or floor areas.

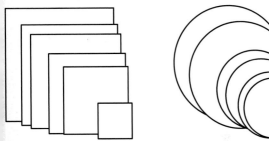

Although any shape could be used, the square and circle are most common as they are the easiest to calculate.

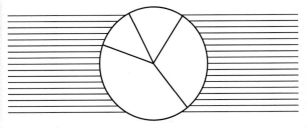

The pie chart is a circular area chart with the whole representing the total value and the segments showing the relative subdivisions. Its resemblance to a pie or cake with slices gives it its name.

## The square area chart

The area of any rectangle is calculated by multiplying the width by the height. To draw squared area charts you simply need to be able to work out square roots and squares of numbers with a calculator. In this example we will construct an area chart showing the relative sizes of Britain, France, Italy, Portugal and Spain.

First, arrange the data in some order, such as descending order by size.

| | |
|---|---|
| France | 547,026 km2 |
| Spain | 504,782 km2 |
| Italy | 301,268 km2 |
| Britain | 244,104 km2 |
| Portugal | 92,082 km2 |

Plot the square for the largest area, France, at a suitable size and calculate the actual area plotted. If we make it 27mm by 27mm the area is 729mm². This represents the land area of 547,026km².

Now you need to calculate the other values in proportion. With the calculator divide 729 by 547,026. This gives an answer of .00133. Use the M+ key to store this in the memory. While the answer is still displayed multiply it by 504,782 then press the square root key. The result, 25.9, is the length of the side of the square for Spain in millimetres. Use the memory readout (MR) key to redisplay the .00133 and multiply it by the other values to obtain the lengths of the sides of each box.

| Value | Plot area | Side |
|---|---|---|
| 547,026 km² | 729.00 | 27.0mm |
| 504,782 km² | 671.36 | 25.9mm |
| 301,268 km² | 400.68 | 20.0mm |
| 244,104 km² | 324.66 | 18.0mm |
| 92,082 km² | 122.47 | 11.1mm |

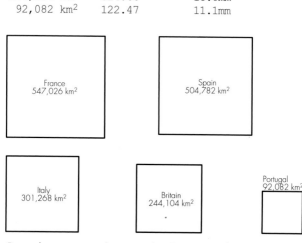

France
547,026 km²

Spain
504,782 km²

Italy
301,268 km²

Britain
244,104 km²

Portugal
92,082 km²

Draw the remaining boxes to the dimensions shown.
The squares show the comparative areas of the countries but the chart does take up a lot of page space.

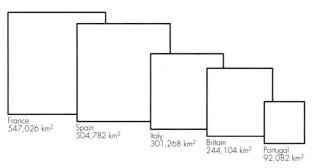

France
547,026 km²

Spain
504,782 km²

Italy
301,268 km²

Britain
244,104 km²

Portugal
92,082 km²

By overlapping the boxes the chart is made more compact, neater and yet still carries the information.
The areas can be overlapped in any satisfactory way as long as enough of each one shows to enable the reader to make the visual comparison.

Overlapping the areas so that they have one common corner makes the chart very compact but still shows the full extent of each area. Use leader lines if labels do not fit on the chart.

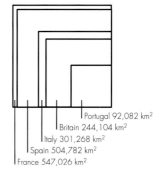

Portugal 92,082 km²

Britain 244,104 km²

Italy 301,268 km²

Spain 504,782 km²

France 547,026 km²

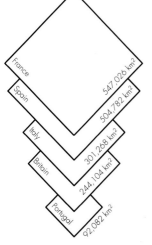

Vertically aligned, rotated squares give a less orthodox look to the chart. This takes up more vertical space but makes labelling each area quite straightforward. The squares are aligned so that the base corner of each is equally spaced apart. This helps emphasize the differences in area of each square.

## Oblong area charts

Oblongs used as area charts require additional calculation.

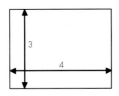

First draw up the largest oblong but make sure that the width to height ratio is simple, such as 1 to 2, or 3 to 4. In this example the rectangle has a proportion of 3 to 4, height to width.

The rectangle measures 21x28mm which gives an area of 588mm$^2$ which represents the area of the largest item in our data set, 31,820 miles$^2$.
Divide 588 by 31,820 to obtain the conversion factor: .0185. Now work out the relative sizes of the other lakes by multiplying the mile areas by .0185 .

```
Lake Superior    31,820 miles²        588
Lake Victoria    26,828 miles²        496
Lake Huron       23,010 miles²        425
Lake Michigan    22,400 miles²        414
```

To calculate the relative width and height of each oblong we use a variation on the formula: area = width x height. As we have used a proportion of 4 to 3, width to height we can restate the formula as follows:

area = width x $^3/_4$ width,  *or*  area = width x .75 width,
*so* area = .75 width$^2$  *therefore*  496 = .75 width$^2$
*therefore* 496 ÷ .75 = width$^2$  *therefore*  661.33 = width$^2$
*therefore*  $\sqrt{661.33}$ = width = 25.7

So the width of the rectangle for Lake Victoria is 25.7mm and the height is .75 of that, 19.27mm. (Check by multiplying the two figures.) Now calculate the other rectangles in proportion.

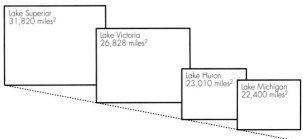

Position the oblongs to fit the design area and add labels.

## Circular area charts

These also require some careful calculation. Choose a suitable size for the largest circle then calculate its actual area by using the formula: area = pi x radius$^2$ (pi is the greek name given to the value 3.142 which is used to calculate the ratio of the circumference of a square to its diameter).

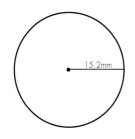

In this example the radius is 15.2mm.

area = 3.142 x 15.2mm$^2$
*therefore* area = 726mm

(This is the same area as that of the largest square in the chart on pages 72 and 73.)

You now need to work out the radii for the other circles by manipulating the formula: area = pi x radius$^2$.
So to calculate the radius of a circle with an area 671mm$^2$:

671 = pi x radius$^2$     *therefore* 671 ÷ pi = radius$^2$
671 ÷ 3.142 = radius$^2$  *therefore* 213.6 = radius$^2$
*therefore* √213.6 = radius = 14.6mm

The radii of the other circles are calculated in the same way.

The layout of the circles in relation to each other is variable but leave room for labels.
Overlapping the circles saves space but still enables a comparison to be made. To space overlapped circles evenly, draw the largest and smallest in their correct positions, using a centre line to align them. Measure the distance between the same point on each of these circles. Divide this amount by one less than the total number of circles. Mark off this distance along the centre line and draw the remaining circles.

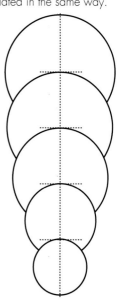

## The pie chart

This is the most common form of area chart. It is frequently used to show a percentage breakdown of a total. Segments may be labelled with their percentage values or may have actual values labelled, or both. When used in a comparative group the pie areas tend to be shown as equal although the total values represented may vary.

To draw a pie chart accurately you will need a circle template, or pair of compasses, and a protractor to measure the angles, in addition to regular drafting tools. You will also need a calculator to convert values to angles.

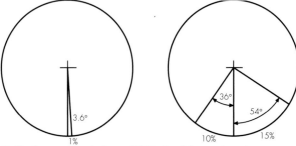

● Circles are divided into 360°. So if the total circle represents 100%, an angle of 3.6° is equal to 1%. So 10% of the circle is 36°; 15% is 54° and so on.

**To convert data to degrees** add up the data; divide 360° by that total; multiply the answer obtained (the factor) by each value in turn. The answers should add up to 360°.

**To convert data to percentages** divide 100 by the data total and multiply each value by that factor.

| Value | Per cent | Angle |
|---|---|---|
| 47 | 18.8% | 68 |
| 43 | 17.2% | 62 |
| 39 | 15.6% | 56 |
| 64 | 25.6% | 92 |
| 57 | 22.8% | 82 |
| 250  (total) | 100% | 360 |

The example shows data based on a total value of 250 divided into segments of 47, 43, 39, 64 and 57. The angles have been rounded to the nearest whole number as fractions of a degree are too small to plot.

**Put the data in order** before plotting the chart. These could be in order of size, in alphabetic order or can follow some other set pattern.

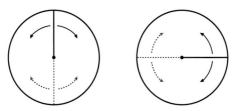

**Choose a starting point** for plotting. This can be vertical (12 or 6 o'clock on a clockface) or horizontal (9 or 3 o'clock). The segments then follow in either clockwise or anticlockwise sequence.

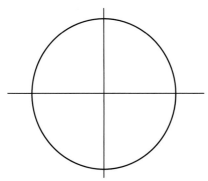

Begin plotting the chart by first drawing a circle to the chosen size for the pie. Mark the centre of the circle and draw a vertical line from the centre through the edge of the circle and extended to just beyond the diameter of the protractor.

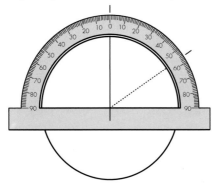

Place the protractor so that its centre cross-hair is exactly over the centre of the circle and the zero point is vertically aligned along the vertical plot line. Mark the first division against the edge of the protractor at the correct angle, 56°.

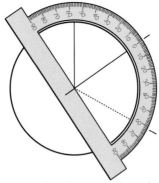

Rotate the protractor to align the zero point with the 56° mark and plot the next angle, 62°. Rotate the protractor to align the zero with that angle, and so on. Keep the lines as fine as possible so that they are clear to read where they converge. When all the lines are plotted check that the last segment is the correct 92° then ink in the chart. Start with the circle as this is the trickiest part to draw.

Add labels to complete the chart keeping them horizontal to ease legibility. When placing them within segments, position them so that they are visually centred. If adjacent to segments place them at the same visual distance from the edge and centre them visually along the arc of each segment.

## Highlighting a segment

A popular way of drawing attention to a particular segment is to separate it from the main chart so it looks like a slice being removed from the pie.

Commence the plot by drawing two concentric circles, the inner one is the edge of the pie and the outer one is the edge of the removed segment.

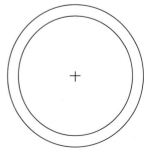

Plot the chart as previously described, remembering to work to the inner circle. Bisect the angle of the required segment (measure the angle and divide by two) and draw a line from the centre of the circle to pass through the bisecting point and through the line of the outer circle.

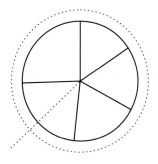

Draw all the chart lines including the sides but not the edge of the offset slice. Slide the tracing along the bisecting line so that the inner circle's edge touches the outer circle. Make sure the centre point sits on the bisecting line. Draw in the outer edge and the sides of the slice.

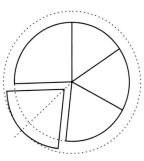

## The exploded pie

It is possible to separate all segments and create an 'exploded' pie chart, but unless the slices are all identical in size, this can look untidy.

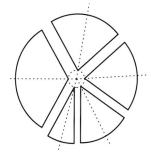

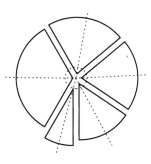

If you make the offset from the centre equal, the spacing of segments will be uneven.

If the spacing between the segments is even, the offset from the centre will have to vary.

### Strengthening a pie chart

Enhance the basic pie graph by adding a dropped shadow. To draw the shadow plot a second circle either directly below or offset to one side of the perimeter of the pie. Ink in that part of the second circle exposed below the first.

A 3-D edge can be added to the basic pie. Plot a semi-circle directly below the perimeter of the pie. Draw vertical lines at either side to connect it to the pie. Add any verticals for segments that abut the lower edge. The thickness of the pie is a matter of choice but should be consistent in a series.

If adding a 3-D edge to a pie with a slice offset you need to add edges to the exposed 'cut'.
Draw the main chart sections in position then slide the trace vertically down a measured amount to plot the edge (including the revealed edges from where the segment is removed).

Put the trace back in the original position then slide it along the bisecting angle line to draw the upper edges of the slice. Then slide it down vertically from this position by exactly the same amount as for the thickness of the main chart.

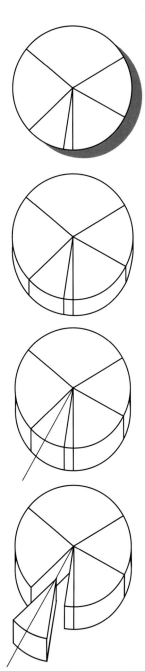

## Getting the chart in perspective

Plotting a pie chart in true perspective would be extremely complex but a perspective effect can be achieved by compressing the circle to form an ellipse. The degree of distortion of the areas of the segments increases as the ellipse is made shallower. When not taken to extremes, the elliptical pie presents a useful way of saving space.

The examples show a pie chart based on the same data plotted on projections of 90° (circle), 60°, 45° and 35°16'.

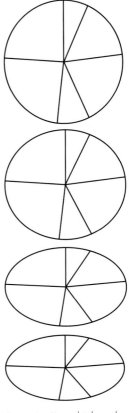

With a 60° ellipse the segments are only slightly distorted but there is a considerable space saving.

At 45° the distortion is more obvious.

The 35° 16' ellipse is drawn with an isometric template. It is probably the shallowest ellipse that should be used.

(It is possible to obtain an isometric protractor which makes plotting the segments of this projection simple.)

● Convert all the data into segment angles first, as if preparing a flat pie chart.

● Don't plot the segment angles directly onto the edge of any ellipse with an ordinary protractor. You have to project the divisions from a full circle onto the circumference of the ellipse.

Start by drawing an ellipse with a template to the required size and draw a horizontal and a vertical rule through the centre extending beyond the circumference of the ellipse. Draw a circle to the width of the ellipse at its widest point. Draw this accurately or it will be impossible to plot any points on the left and right edges.

With a protractor mark out the angles for each segment and transfer these to the edge of the circle – not directly onto the ellipse.

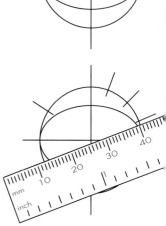

Using a set-square and ruler, draw lines parallel to the vertical guide from the points on the circle to cut the circumference of the ellipse. Make sure that points close to the ends of the ellipse fall above the horizontal line if above on the circle or below if below on the circle.

The points on the ellipse circumference can now be joined to the centre to complete the plot.
Take extra care when inking in to avoid congestion where lines converge on the centre point.

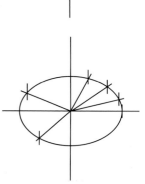

The elliptical pie benefits from the addition of a 3D edge. This is drawn by adding a second, lower semi-ellipse directly below the pie. Make sure the lower ellipse is parallel to the first.

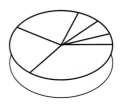

Construct vertical lines from the points along the front edge of the pie to the lower line. Finally draw vertical lines from the edges of the lower ellipse to the pie to form the sides.

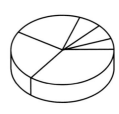

The depth of the pie can be variable but foremost segments on a deeper pie will have more impact as they have more visible surface area.

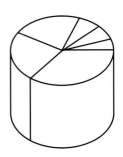

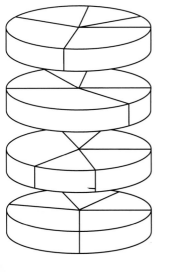

### Stacking pies

Ovelapping pies is a useful way of saving space .Keep the depths of the pies and the space separating them consistent. Make sure that the overlap does not obscure too much of the back segments. Too much overlap will also give undue prominence to the front segments. Plan the chart carefully giving particular attention to fitting labels into the reduced surface of the chart.

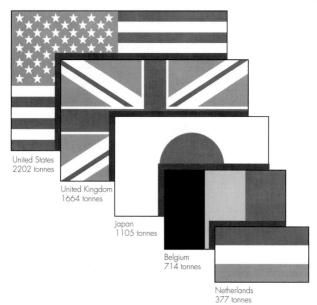

United States
2202 tonnes

United Kingdom
1664 tonnes

Japan
1105 tonnes

Belgium
714 tonnes

Netherlands
377 tonnes

*Above* Oblong area chart using flags to identify countries.

*Opposite: Top* Pie chart based on coin.
　　　　*Middle* Double pie with combined labels.
　　　　*Bottom* Combined pie and double bar chart.

*Below* Combined area and pie chart.

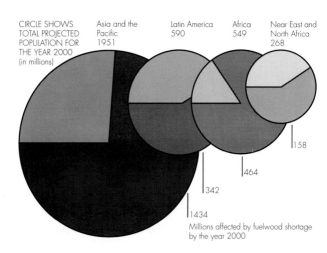

CIRCLE SHOWS
TOTAL PROJECTED
POPULATION FOR
THE YEAR 2000
(in millions)

Asia and the
Pacific
1951

Latin America
590

Africa
549

Near East and
North Africa
268

158

464

342

1434

Millions affected by fuelwood shortage
by the year 2000

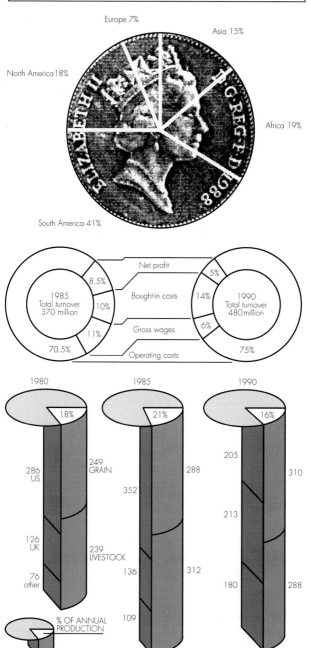

Europe 7%

Asia 15%

North America 18%

Africa 19%

South America 41%

Net profit

1985
Total turnover
370 million

8.5%

10%

11%

70.5%

Bought-in costs

Gross wages

Operating costs

1990
Total turnover
480 million

5%

14%

6%

75%

1980

1985

1990

18%

21%

16%

286
US

249
GRAIN

126
UK

76
other

239
LIVESTOCK

352

136

109

288

312

205

213

180

310

288

% OF ANNUAL
PRODUCTION

ORIGIN        TYPE

| Length | | |
|---|---|---|
| | centimetre (cm)<br>1 cm = 0.3937 in | inch (in)<br>1 in = 2.5400 cm |
| | metre (m)<br>1 m = 3.2808 ft | foot (ft)<br>1 ft = 0.3048 m |
| | metre (m)<br>1 m = 1.0936 yd | yard (yd)<br>1 yd = 0.9144 m |
| | kilometre (km)<br>1 km = 0.6214 mi | mile (mi)<br>1 mi = 1.6093 km |

| Area | | |
|---|---|---|
| | square centimetre ($cm^2$)<br>1 $cm^2$ = 0.1550 $in^2$ | square inch ($in^2$)<br>1 $in^2$ = 6.4516 $cm^2$ |
| | hectare (ha)<br>1 ha = 2.4711 a | acre (a)<br>1 a = 0.4047 ha |
| | square metre ($m^2$)<br>1 $m^2$ = 10.7639 $ft^2$ | square foot ($ft^2$)<br>1 $ft^2$ = 0.0929 $m^2$ |
| | square metre ($m^2$)<br>1 $m^2$ = 1.1960 $yd^2$ | square yard ($yd^2$)<br>1 $yd^2$ = 0.8361 $m^2$ |
| | square kilometre ($km^2$)<br>1 $km^2$ = 0.3861 $mi^2$ | square mile ($mi^2$)<br>1 $mi^2$ = 2.5900 $km^2$ |

| Volume | | |
|---|---|---|
| | cubic centimetre ($cm^3$)<br>1 $cm^3$ = 0.0610 $in^3$ | cubic inch ($in^3$)<br>1 $in^3$ = 16.3871 $cm^3$ |
| | cubic metre ($m^3$)<br>1 $m^3$ = 35.3147 $ft^3$ | cubic foot ($ft^3$)<br>1 $ft^3$ = 0.0283 $m^3$ |
| | cubic metre ($m^3$)<br>1 $m^3$ = 1.3080 $yd^3$ | cubic yard ($yd^3$)<br>1 $yd^3$ = 0.7646 $m^3$ |

| Weight | | |
|---|---|---|
| | gram (g)<br>1 g = 0.0353 ozs | ounce (oz)<br>1 oz = 28.3495 g |
| | kilogram (kg)<br>1 kg = 2.2046 lbs | pound (lb)<br>1 lb = 0.4536 kg |
| | tonne (t)<br>1 t = 1.1023 short tons | short ton – 2000lbs<br>1 short ton = 0.9072 t |
| | tonne (t)<br>1 t = 0.9842 long tons | long ton – 2240lbs<br>1 long ton = 1.0160 t |
| Liquid measure | centilitre (cl)<br>1 cl = 0.3520 fl. oz | UK fluid ounce (fl. oz)<br>1 fl. oz = 2.8413 cl |
| | centilitre (cl)<br>1 cl = 0.3381 fl. oz | US fluid ounce (fl. oz)<br>1 fl. oz = 2.9574 cl |
| | litre (l)<br>1 l = 1.7598 pt | UK pint (pt)<br>1 pt = 0.5683 l |
| | litre (l)<br>1 l = 2.1134 pt | US pint (pt)<br>1 pt = 0.4732 l |
| | litre (l)<br>1 l = 0.2200 gal | UK gallon (gal)<br>1 gal = 4.5460 l |
| | litre (l)<br>1 l = 0.2642 gal | US gallon (gal)<br>1 gal = 3.7854 l |
| Speed | kilometres per hour (kmph)<br>1 kmph = 0.6214 mph | miles per hour (mph)<br>1 mph = 1.6093 kmph |

To convert measurements, multiply the value by the conversion factor shown above. For example, to convert 7,250 pounds to kilograms multiply 7250 by 0.4536 (=3288.60kg). Also shown above are acceptable abbreviations (although house styles may vary).

## ACKNOWLEDGMENTS

**Series editor:** Judy Martin
**Art Direction:** Nigel Osborne
**Design:** Trevor Bounford
**Artwork:** Denise Goodey, Justin Ives and
Nicholas Rowland